# FIFTY YEARS AGO

# Having Fun

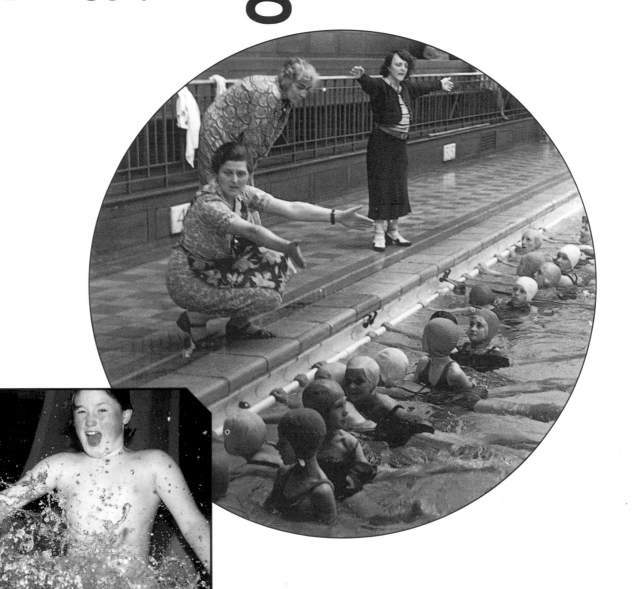

Karen Bryant-Mole

WAYLAND

Titles in the series
**At Home**
**Going on a Trip**
**Having Fun**
**In the High Street**

**All Wayland books encourage children to read and help them improve their literacy.**

✓ The contents page, page numbers, headings and index help locate specific pieces of information.

✓ The glossary reinforces alphabetic knowledge and extends vocabulary.

✓ The further information section suggests other books dealing with the same subject.

✓ Find out more about how this book is specifically relevant to the National Literacy Strategy on page 31.

Editor: Carron Brown
Consultant: Norah Granger
Cover design: White Design
Inside design: Michael Leaman
Production controller: Carol Titchener

First published in 1998 by
Wayland Publishers Limited,
61 Western Road, Hove,
East Sussex BN3 1JD

Typeset in England by
Michael Leaman Design Partnership
Printed and bound in Italy by L.G. Canale &
C.S.p.A Turin

British Library in Cataloguing Data
Bryant-Mole, Karen
    Having Fun. – (Fifty years ago)
    1. Family recreation – Great Britain – History
    – 20th century – Juvenile literature
    2. Great Britain – Social conditions – 1945
    – Juvenile literature
    3. Great Britain – Social life and customs –
    1945 – Juvenile literature
    I. Title 941'. 085

ISBN 0705 23944

Picture acknowledgements
The publishers would like to thank the following
for allowing their pictures to be used in this book:
Corbis UK cover; Getty Images 5, 9, 11, 15, 19, 23,
25; Topham Picturepoint 7, 13, 17, 21; Wayland
Picture Library/ Stuart Weir *cover* [inset], 6, 8,
10, 12, 14, 16, 20, 22, 24.

# CONTENTS

Circus 4

Holidays 6

Birthdays 8

Playground 10

Dancing 12

Swimming 14

Fairground 16

Bonfire Night 18

Playing 20

Watching Sport 22

Playing Sport 24

At the Cinema 26

Notes for parents and teachers 28

About the photographs 29

Glossary 30

Further information,
including literacy information 31

Index 32

In this book we are introduced to the Maynard family. We will meet Mr and Mrs Maynard, their children Tom and Emma, and Tom and Emma's grandparents John and Margaret. Compare how they enjoy themselves with other families having fun fifty years ago.

# These acrobats are performing in front of the audience.

All the acts in this circus are performed by people. There are jugglers, tightrope walkers, clowns, acrobats and trapeze artists. The performers travel all around the world.

# FIFTY YEARS AGO

## These performers and their elephants practised their act before the show.

A long time ago, most circuses had performing animals. As well as elephants, there were often sea lions, bears, tigers and lions. Many people today think it is wrong to see wild animals perform tricks.

## I remember...

**Margaret Maynard is Tom and Emma's grandmother. She remembers how excited all the children were when the circus came to town. 'A few days before the circus arrived, posters advertising the circus were stuck up. Then the huge circus tent went up. The animals lived in cages. I remember the smell from the cages being really strong.**

# The Maynard family are going to Portugal for a holiday.

Portugal is thousands of kilometres away from the Maynards' home. The Maynards are flying to Portugal by plane. They will stay in a hotel near the beach. Mr and Mrs Maynard are looking forward to the hot, sunny weather. Tom and Emma can't wait to go to the children's club.

# These children had their holiday in England.

Fifty years ago, most people did not go abroad for their holidays. Instead, a lot of people went to the seaside. Donkey rides along the beach were very popular.

## I remember...

**John Maynard is Tom and Emma's grandfather. When he was a boy, he used to stay in a seaside guest house. 'One year, it did nothing but rain all week. We had to leave the guest house after breakfast and couldn't come back until tea-time. It was too cold and wet to go on the beach, so I spent most of the week playing the slot machines in the penny arcade.'**

# BIRTHDAYS

## Tom is having a birthday party at a sports centre.

Tom decided to have his birthday party here because he and his friends really enjoy sport. There are lots of activities for the children. Tom's mum and dad bring party food for the children to eat afterwards.

# This girl had her birthday party at home.

Fifty years ago, most children had their birthday parties at home. They usually played party games such as Blind Man's Buff, Hunt the Thimble and O'Grady Says.

## I remember...

John enjoyed birthday parties but he didn't enjoy getting ready for them. 'My mum used to make me wear my best clothes. She scrubbed my face clean and brushed my hair so hard I thought it would fall out. Then she put some of dad's hair cream on my hair to make it shiny and keep it flat.'

# PLAYGROUND

## Emma enjoys playing in adventure playgrounds.

Emma likes pretending that this wobbly bridge is in the jungle. She pretends that if she falls off, she might get eaten by crocodiles. If she really fell off, she wouldn't get hurt because there is a soft surface underneath the bridge.

# This child liked to play on the swings.

Most playgrounds were covered in concrete. If a child fell off the swing he or she could have been badly hurt. Today, safety is very important.

## I remember...

Margaret liked to play on the slide when she went to the playground. 'I liked the slide because it was scary and exciting at the same time. It felt so high up and it was such a long way to the ground. Once, I went so fast I shot right off the end.'

# DANCING

## Emma and Tom enjoy going to a disco at their school.

Discos are fun. You can dance with a big group of friends or with one friend. You can even dance by yourself. The music is very loud. It is usually quite dark with flashing lights.

# These children learned to do ballroom dancing.

When grown-ups went to dances fifty years ago, they usually did ballroom dancing. They did special dances like the waltz and the foxtrot. Each dance had its own steps and music. You danced with a partner.

## I remember...

John hated ballroom dancing when he was a boy. 'Every Saturday morning I had to go to ballroom dancing lessons. I was useless. My partner was a girl called Gwen. I was always standing on her feet.'

# SWIMMING

## Tom is sliding down the slide at the swimming pool.

The Maynard family all go swimming on Friday evenings. Emma likes the wave machine. After they have been swimming they have a hot shower. Then they have a drink and some crisps at the swimming pool cafe.

# The girls in this picture had swimming lessons.

Fifty years ago, swimming pools were usually called swimming baths. There were no slides or wave machines. The buildings were not warm and it felt chilly when you got out of the water.

## I remember...

Margaret learned to swim when she was eight years old. 'I had a really strict teacher called Mrs Hunt. We were so scared of her that we did exactly what we were told. When she said swim, we swam.'

# FAIRGROUND

## The Maynards are enjoying a ride at a theme park.

Tom's favourite ride at the park is the big dipper. It makes his stomach feel funny as he goes up and down. Sophie likes the ride in a boat. It hurtles down a hill and splashes through some water.

## These children liked to ride on the merry-go-round.

This ride was part of a travelling fair that went to different towns and villages. As well as rides there would have been side-shows, such as hoop-la, and fortune-tellers. Today, fairground rides are faster and more exciting.

### I remember...

John remembers when the fair came to his town. 'We couldn't wait for school to end when the fair was in town. My friend, Jack, had his fortune told one year. The fortune teller said he would get married and have three children. We all laughed but twenty years later, Jack had a wife and three kids.'

# BONFIRE NIGHT

## These people are watching a fireworks display.

The Maynards always go to a big firework display on Bonfire Night. Everybody must buy a ticket to get in. This money is spent on fantastic fireworks. The Maynards like going to a display because it is safe and well organised.

## This girl lit the fireworks in her back garden.

In the past, many people were badly burned by fireworks. Today, there is a firework code that tells people how to use fireworks safely. Children should never be allowed to light fireworks.

### I remember...

Margaret remembers one bonfire party she went to. 'We were eating toffee apples and having a lovely time. Then some of the boys lit some fireworks called Jumping Jacks. They were firecrackers that jumped all around the place. One of them jumped into my brother's boot by accident. I'd never heard anyone scream so loud. He's still got the scars from the burns.'

# Tom and Emma love playing computer games.

Tom and Emma have lots of toys. They like playing with construction sets to build moving machines. They also have an electric car racing set.

## This little girl liked playing with her toy doll.

Fifty years ago, children had fewer toys than they do now. But, just as today, toys were often like the things that children saw around them. Doll's prams were just like real prams. Toy trains looked like actual steam trains.

### I remember...

Margaret had a toy tea-set. 'My tea set was made out of china. It had pink roses on it, just like the real tea set my mum and dad had. I used to have pretend tea parties with my doll who was called Heather and my teddy who was called Albert.'

# WATCHING SPORT

## Today, people can watch sport from all around the world on their televisions.

The Maynards all have their own favourite sport which they like to watch. Mrs Maynard likes watching the skiing. Mr Maynard enjoys watching motor racing. Tom likes American football. Emma's favourite sport is basketball.

# FIFTY YEARS AGO

## This crowd of supporters enjoyed watching their football team.

Fifty years ago, only a few people had televisions. If they wanted to watch sport, they went to sports grounds. Every Saturday afternoon in winter, thousands of people went to football matches.

### I remember...

Margaret's family always supported their local football team. 'Whenever our team was playing at home, the whole family went to watch. It was always crowded. Fortunately, people let children go to the front so we could see properly. When our team scored a goal, the crowd roared.'

# PLAYING SPORT

## Emma enjoys doing judo.

Emma goes to a judo club every week. She enjoys judo because it is fun and it keeps her fit. It might look rough but the idea is to get the opponent on the mat without hurting him or her.

## Boxing used to be a popular sport for boys.

Not many boys do boxing as a sport today. Boxers often get punched in the head. They can get badly injured. Today, many boxers wear head guards to protect them.

### I remember...

John used to like playing sport. 'I was really sporty. Hockey, football, cricket – you name it, I did it. I never did boxing. A lot of people thought it was a good sport for boys. They thought it kept them out of trouble and used up their energy.

# AT THE CINEMA

## The Maynards are going to the cinema to watch a film together.

There are lots of different screens at this cinema, so there is usually a film that all the family will like. Before they sit down, they usually buy some drinks and a big box of popcorn.

## These children used to watch films by themselves.

On Saturday mornings, many cinemas had special children's shows. The children were brought to the cinema by their parents and left there to enjoy the films.

### I remember...

Margaret used to go to the cinema every Saturday morning. 'Every week there was a film, a cartoon and a serial that carried on from one week to the next. We really enjoyed it. It was very noisy. We all cheered the goodies and booed the baddies.'

# NOTES FOR PARENTS

**This book is designed to be used on many different levels.**

The words in bold provide a simple, core text. The rest of the text provides greater detail, more background information and some personal reminiscences. Competent readers will be able to tackle the entire text themselves. Younger readers could share the reading of the text with an adult. Non-readers will benefit from hearing the text read aloud to them.

All children will enjoy comparing and contrasting the main pictures on each double page spread. Every picture is a rich resource with much that can be observed and discussed. Ideas for discussion points and questions to ask about each photograph can be found below.

Children are likely to have relatives who will have clear memories of everyday life fifty years ago. There is nothing that brings history to life more vividly than personal recollections. If these memories can be supported by photographs or other artefacts, such as letters, toys or other objects, then the experience is made all the more 'real' to a child.

This particular book is about having fun. You could encourage children to think about the things they enjoy doing and to consider the similarities and differences between the ways in which children have fun today and the ways in which they had fun fifty years ago. In many instances, the sort of activity has remained the same, such as going on holiday or playing with toys, but the type of places visited or actual toys played with have changed significantly.

## About the Photographs

### Circus p 5

*Questions to ask*
How can you tell that this is just a rehearsal and not a performance?
What type of elephants are these?

*Points to explore*
Discuss the issues surrounding performing animals.
Consider what life might have been like for children in a travelling circus.

### Holidays  p 7

*Questions to ask*
Do you think this picture was taken on a hot, sunny day?
Do the donkeys look as though they are enjoying themselves?

*Points to explore*
Find out about other beach entertainment, such as Punch and Judy shows.
Talk about the reasons why fewer people took their holidays abroad fifty years ago.

### Birthdays  p 9

*Questions to ask*
Do the children in the photograph look older or younger than you?
How are the clothes different to the sort of clothes you might wear today?

*Points to explore*
Find out how popular party games of the time were played.
What kinds of presents did children give to each other.

### Playground p11

*Questions to ask*
Does this playground look very busy?
What is the seat of this swing made from?

*Points to explore*
Find out about the different surfaces that are used in playgrounds today to make them safer places to play.
Ask friends and relatives what they played on in playgrounds fifty years ago.

## Dancing  p 13

*Questions to ask*
Do the children in the photograph look happy?
Does ballroom dancing look easy?

*Points to explore*
Listen to the types of music that went with the
different ballroom dances.
Find out about the clothes that adults wore to go ballroom dancing.

## Swimming  p 15

*Questions to ask*
How many children can you see in this photograph?
How many of them are wearing swimming caps?

*Points to explore*
Find out where else people went swimming, e.g. rivers
and lidos.
Discover what was fashionable in swimwear fifty years ago.

## Fairground  p17

*Questions to ask*
How fast do you think this merry-go-round is going?
What kind of pretend vehicles do you think these chil-
dren are driving?

*Points to explore*
Find out if any travelling fairs used to visit your area.
Ask friends and relatives what rides and side-shows
they remember seeing at fairs fifty years ago.

## Bonfire Night  p 19

*Questions to ask*
Can you describe this girl's clothing?
What is dangerous about her actions?

*Points to explore*
Research the story of Guy Fawkes and Bonfire Night.
Find out about the Firework Code.

## Playing  p 21

*Questions to ask*
How old do you think this little girl is?
Do you think her doll looks cheap or expensive?

*Points to explore*
Find out about other toys that children played with
fifty years ago.
Explore the materials that toys are made from and
notice how they have changed over the years.

## Watching sport  p 23

*Questions to ask*
What are the fans wearing ?
What mood are the supporters in?

*Points to explore*
Find out whether your local league football team was
a top team fifty years ago.
Discuss the changes to sports clothes in recent years.

## Playing sport  p 25

*Questions to ask*
How many boys and how many girls can you see in the
photograph?
Are the boys' heads and bodies protected in any way?

*Points to explore*
Which sports were popular fifty years ago but not now
Think of popular sports today which didn't exist fifty
years ago, e.g. windsurfing.

## At the Cinema  p 27

Questions to ask
Do you think it was warm or cold in this cinema?
What are the expressions on the children's faces.like?

Points to explore
Discuss popular movie stars from fifty years ago.
Consider other forms of entertainment from that time.

# GLOSSARY

 **big dipper** A fairground ride, with train-type carriages that run on tracks.

 **hoop-la** A fairground game where hoops are thrown over prizes. If the hoop lands around the prize, you win it.

 **circus tent** The huge tent where the circus is performed, sometimes called a big top.

 **merry-go-round** A fairground ride, sometimes also called a roundabout or a carousel.

 **doll's pram** This doll's pram looks like real prams did fifty years ago.

 **steam train** This toy steam train looks like the real trains of fifty years ago.

 **guest house** A small hotel where bed, breakfast and an evening meal are provided.

 **toffee apple** An apple on a stick, coated in hot toffee that has been left to cool.

 **hair cream** A sort of lotion that is combed through the hair to make it shiny.

 **trapeze artist** Someone who does circus tricks hanging from swinging bars, high up in the circus tent.

# FURTHER INFORMATION

*People Having Fun* by K. Bryant-Mole
(People through History series - Wayland, 1996)

*Toys* by K. Bryant-Mole (History from Objects series - Wayland, 1994)

*Toys discovered through History* (Linkers series - A & C Black, 1996)

*Seaside* by R. Thomson  (Changing Times - Watts, 1994)

*Toys and Games* by R. Thomson (Changing Times series - Watts, 1994)

*Having Fun in Grandma's Day* by F. Gardner
(In Grandma's Day - Evans, 1997)

**Use this book for teaching literacy**

This book can help you in the literacy hour in the following ways:

✓ Children can extend the skills of reading non-fiction. There are two levels of text given, a simple version and a more advanced level.

✓ They can recognise that non-fiction books with similar themes can present similar information in different ways.

✓ They can be encouraged to ask their relatives about their lives when they were children and learn indirectly about history.

✓ They can imagine and write stories about how they would have had fun fifty years ago, for example.

# INDEX

**Aa**  animals 5

**Bb**  ballroom dancing 13
birthdays 8, 9
Bonfire Night 18, 19
boxing 25

**Cc**  cartoons 27
cinemas 26, 27
circuses 4, 5
clothes 9

**Dd**  dancing 12, 13
discos 12
dolls 21

**Ee**

**Ff**  fairgrounds 17
films 26, 27
fireworks 18, 19
food 7, 8, 14, 26
football 22, 23, 25
fortune tellers 17

**Gg**  games 9, 20
guest houses 7

**Hh**  holidays 6, 7
homes 6, 9

**Ii**

**Jj**  judo 24

**Kk**

**Ll**  lessons 13, 15

**Mm**  merry-go-rounds 17
music 12, 13

**Nn**

**Oo**

**Pp**  parties 8, 9, 19
performers 4, 5
playgrounds 10, 11
playing 10, 11, 20, 21

**Qq**

**Rr**

**Ss**  schools 12
seaside 7
serials 27

side-shows 17
slides 11, 14, 15
sport 8, 22, 23, 24, 25
supporters 23
swimming 14, 15
swings 11

**Tt**  tea-sets 21
teddies 21
televisions 22, 23
theme parks 16
toffee apples 19
toys 20, 21

**Uu**

**Vv**

**Ww**

**Xx**

**Yy**

**Zz**